YOGA

IN A NUTSHELL

YOGA
A STEP-BY-STEP GUIDE

ANNIE JONES

TED SMART

First published in
Great Britain in 1998 by
ELEMENT BOOKS LIMITED
Shaftesbury, Dorset, SP7 8BP

Published in the USA in
1998 by
ELEMENT BOOKS INC
160 North Washington
Street, Boston,
MA 02114

Published in
Australia in 1998 by
ELEMENT BOOKS LIMITED
and distributed by Penguin Australia Ltd.
487 Maroondah Highway, Ringwood,
Victoria 3134

Reprinted September 1998, March 1999,
June 1999

NOTE FROM THE PUBLISHER

Any information given in this book is not intended to be taken as a replacement for medical advice. Any person with a condition requiring medical attention should consult a qualified practitioner or therapist.

Designed and created with
The Bridgewater Book Company Ltd

ELEMENT BOOKS LIMITED
Managing Editor Miranda Spicer
Senior Commissioning Editor Caro Ness
Project Editor Katie Worrall
Production Manager Susan Sutterby
Production Controller Claire Legg

THE BRIDGEWATER BOOK
COMPANY LIMITED

Art Director Terry Jeavons
Designer Glyn Bridgewater
Managing Editor Anne Townley
Project Manager Fiona Corbridge
Photography Ian Parsons
Picture Research Lynda Marshall
Page layout Glyn Bridgewater
Three-dimensional models Mark Jamieson
Illustrations Andrew Kulman

Printed and bound by
Dai Nippon Printing Co.,(HK) Ltd.

British Library Cataloguing in
Publication data available

Library of Congress
Cataloging
in Publication data
available

ISBN 0-00-764005-6

The publishers wish to thank the following for the use of pictures: Bridgeman Art Library: 8B, 9T; e.t. archive: 14; Hulton Deutsch: 17R; Hutchinson: 9B, 9C; Michael Yamashita: 13T; Zefa: 6, 8T, 12T, 16L, 18B, 49

Thanks to:
Annie Jones, Regina Doerstel and Rebecca Goodchild *for help with photography*

Special thanks to:
Regina Doerstel, senior tutor for the LFTS Dru Yoga Diploma course, *for her invaluable contribution and expertise.* A.J.

Contents

What is yoga?

THE WORD YOGA MEANS *"unity" or "oneness," and is derived from the Sanskrit word "yug," which means to join. In spiritual terms it refers to the union of the individual consciousness with the universal consciousness.*

ABOVE ***Use yoga to escape to an island of calm in the stressful sea of everyday life!***

On a practical level, yoga is a means of balancing and harmonizing the body, mind and emotions and is a tool that allows us to withdraw from the chaos of the world and find a quiet space within. It utilizes the innate life force within the body and teaches us how to tap into, harness and direct it skillfully. To achieve this, yoga uses movement, breath, posture, relaxation, and meditation in order to establish a healthy, vibrant, and balanced approach to living.

There are many different branches of yoga, each one designed to meet the needs of different individual personalities. They include Raja, Hatha, Jnana, Karma, Bhakti, Mantra, Laya and Kundalini, to name just a few. Each of us needs to find the style of yoga suited to our particular personality.

We need to find a way of channeling negative emotions and mental stresses out of ourselves if we are to feel peaceful in a chaotic world. By performing the recommended postures in a well-rounded

ABOVE *Yoga does not only produce physical benefits. It also promotes relaxation and emotional balance.*

practice, it is possible to release the anxieties and frustrations that can build up inside as a result of our stressful lifestyle.

Yoga is neither political nor religious, having no dogma whatsoever and an almost universal appeal. Anyone can practice it, irrespective of age, cast, creed or color.

THE BENEFITS OF YOGA

- Relaxes mind and body
- Stretches and tones
- Improves muscle joint mobility
- Improves flexibility
- Improves breathing disorders
- Improves heart conditions
- Strengthens the spine, eases back pain
- Soothes the nervous system
- Stimulates the endocrine system
- Improves digestive disorders
- Relieves tiredness
- Supports and helps ME, MS, the menopause, PMT and stress-related conditions

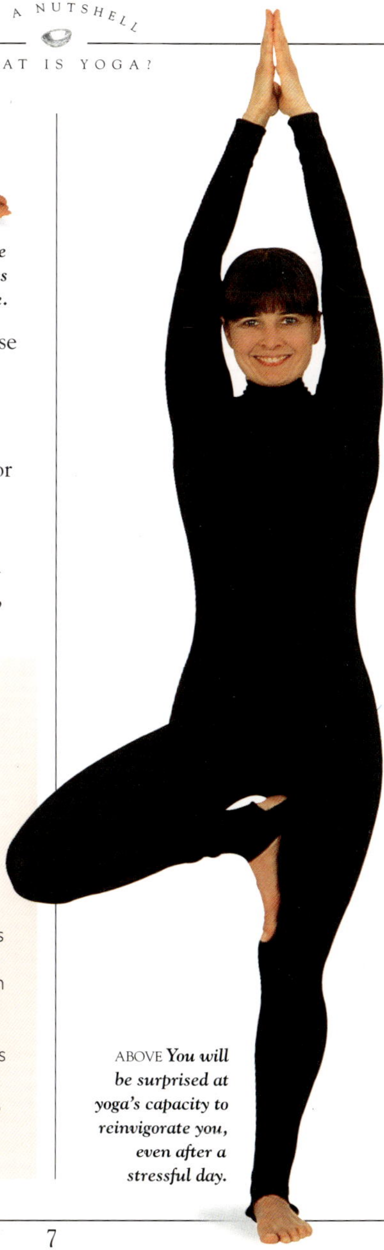

ABOVE *You will be surprised at yoga's capacity to reinvigorate you, even after a stressful day.*

A short history

ABOVE: ***The beauties of nature reflect the aims of yoga: achieving perfect harmony between mind and body.***

YOGA IS SAID to have first appeared in India and other parts of the world over 10,000 years ago. Archeological excavations made in the Indus Valley, in Harapa and Mahanjedaro, uncovered images of Lord Shiva, said to be the founder of yoga, and Paravati, his first student, in various postures and meditation positions.

Some traditions say that yoga was a divine gift received by the ancient sages and offered to humanity as a means of discovering its real nature. Others have suggested that yoga emerged as a direct result of observing nature and the natural laws and attempting to achieve the same perfect balance. Originally, yoga was kept completely secret, passed on only by word of mouth from teacher to disciple. The great sage Patanjali, known as the father of yoga, was the first person to put the knowledge into a form that could be written down. He created the "Eight Limbs of Yoga," which have served as a perfect and undisputed guide ever since and highlight the need to control the mind and desires before practicing the art. Another leading light on yoga was Swatmarama, who wrote the *Hatha Yoga Pradipika*. His particular emphasis was on body control as the ultimate means to control the mind. Today yoga continues to be a unique and powerful means of enhancing and developing the body, mind and emotions, just as it was all those years ago. Modern

ABOVE: ***Patanjali wrote the first guide to the practice of yoga.***

LEFT: ***Lord Shiva, the founder of yoga, teaches his student Paravati a yoga posture.***

yogis, such as Ramakrishna, Vivekananda, and Mahatma Gandhi, have become living examples of this practice in the modern world. Yoga has stood the test of time and will continue to prove itself as an aid to self-development for generations to come. Why? Because it works!

ABOVE: ***A small group, where the teacher is able to give individual attention, is the best way to learn.***

RIGHT: ***An Indian yogi (master of yoga). Yoga is part of the Hindu religious tradition.***

ANCIENT TEXTS OF YOGA

- *The four Vedas*
- *The 108 Upanishads*
- Patanjali's *Yoga Sutras*
- Swatmarama's *Hatha Yoga Pradipika*
- *The Bhagavad Gita* by Veda Vyasa

How does yoga work?

YOGA CAN ALLEVIATE *many of the problems we face today. The postures keep the body tension-free and the controlled breathing keeps the emotions balanced and clear.*

ABOVE: ***The Eagle posture counteracts stiffness and keeps joints supple.***

There are six main groups of yoga postures: standing, inverted, twist, back bend, forward bend, and side bend.

ABOVE: ***The Fish posture is good exercise for asthma sufferers.***

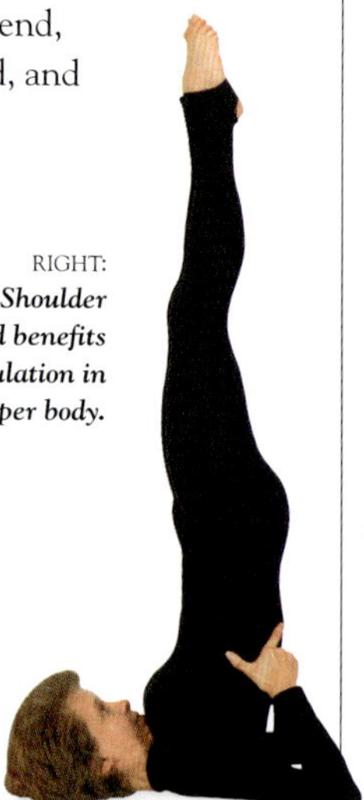

RIGHT: ***The Shoulder Stand benefits circulation in the upper body.***

ABOVE: ***The Back-stretching posture keeps the spine supple.***

BELOW: ***The Lying Twist strengthens the muscles of the abdomen and lower back.***

RIGHT: ***The Triangle posture stretches leg, back and neck.***

- **Standing** Improves efficiency of the muscular, circulatory, respiratory, digestive, reproductive, endocrine, and nervous systems.
- **Inverted** Balances the endocrine system and metabolism. Enhances thinking power and revitalizes the internal organs.
- **Twist** Aids digestion. Helps relieve back pain. Improves intercostal breathing.
- **Back bend** Invigorating. Encourages deep breathing.
- **Forward bend** Improves the blood circulation. Aids digestion. Calms the emotions.
- **Side bend** Stimulates the main organs, for example liver, kidney, stomach, spleen.

In yoga the body is gently and skillfully maneuvred in all directions. Consequently every muscle is stretched and toned. The internal organs are massaged, squeezed, and expanded, improving their general function. The skeletal system is flexed, extended, rotated, and twisted, creating greater joint mobility. The spine is encouraged to maintain a healthy, upright, and pain-free condition. The circulation is improved. The breathing capacity and elasticity of the lungs is enhanced.

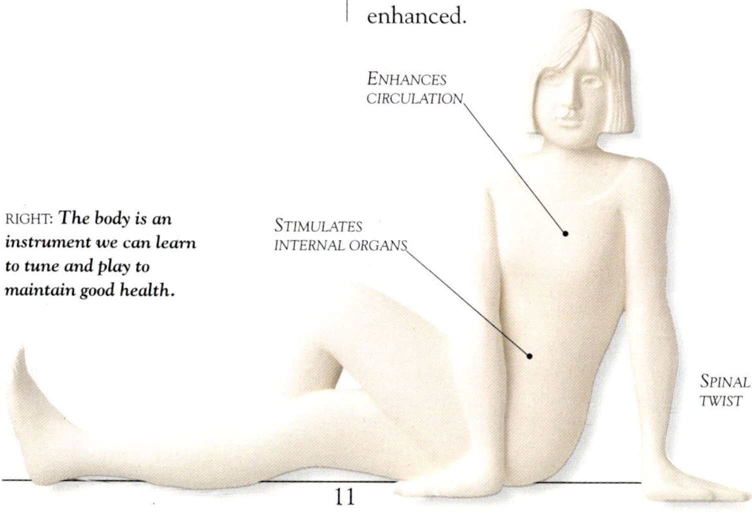

RIGHT: ***The body is an instrument we can learn to tune and play to maintain good health.***

Meditation ~ the ultimate aim of yoga

CONTROL OF THE MIND is the key to success in life. If we can become the master of this dynamic and vast source of potential energy, we have access to a powerful resource.

ABOVE: ***Chanting is one way of focusing the mind and cutting out extraneous thoughts.***

There are as many ways to control the mind, however, as there are individuals seeking the experience of self-mastery. The good news is that there is a way for you. It may be through breath awareness, visualization, candle-gazing, mantra (focusing on a word) or even chanting. The choice is vast …

Traditionally the goal of meditation is said to be to provide a means of uniting individual spirit with universal spirit. In order to achieve this, the mind, body, and breath are disciplined, refined, and perfected by psycho-physiological techniques which also serve as a means of improving health, relaxation, peace of mind, and self-mastery.

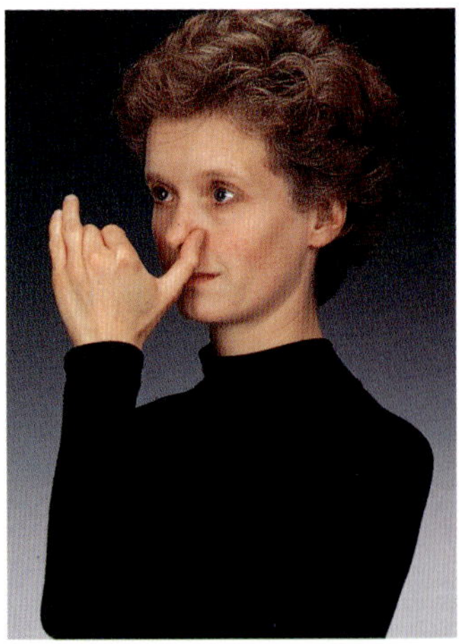

ABOVE: ***Alternate Nostril Breathing is calming and helps relaxation. It also develops awareness of the body.***

ABOVE: ***Meditation in the office.***

Not surprisingly, meditation is undergoing a phenomenal revival as the benefits for de-stressing and relaxing the mind become well known. As well as developing positive emotional health, meditation is a perfect tool for self-transformation.

MEDITATION

- Calms the mind
- Soothes the nervous system
- Balances the right and left hemispheres of the brain
- Gives perspective and clarity
- Gives a sense of purpose
- Improves confidence
- Improves energy levels
- Improves memory

Energy pathways

THE BODY IS A *living miracle, made up of much more than just the physical element. There are in fact five main "bodies" – physical, energetic, emotional, intellectual, and spiritual. Within the practice of yoga it is possible to access and balance all these different levels simultaneously, creating a complete homeostasis and feeling of well-being.*

It is traditionally believed in yoga that there are very powerful energy centers, known as "chakras," within the body. These are said to correspond to the endocrine glands. These energy centers control and affect the way we relate to and communicate with our world. Through practicing postures and breathing techniques, it is possible to influence the way we feel, think, speak, and act, and to overcome different physical and emotional conditions.

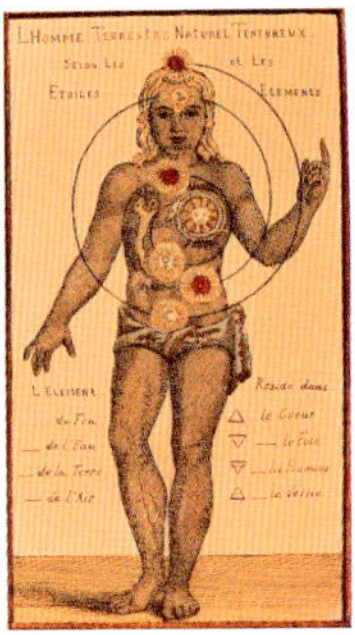

ABOVE: ***An ancient text depicting the energy centers in the body.***

It is said that, in this age, we function primarily from the three lower centers (from the navel level down to the base of the spine). These centers are concerned with the survival impulses as well as with desire and pride. There are specific movements and breathing techniques that help to maintain a focus in the heart center and to develop more positive emotional qualities, such as loving kindness, selfless giving, forgiveness, and not being judgmental.

The aim of yoga is to balance these centers in order to create an effective, compassionate, and confident individual. In a nutshell, yoga simply puts us back in charge of our life.

THE ENERGY PATHWAYS

The Energy Centers	Description of Energy Centers	Balance	Imbalance
Sahasrara	The Thousand-Petalled Lotus Center	Oneness	None
Ajna	The Command Center	Clarity	Confusion
Vishuddhi	The Great Purity Center	Communication	Ineffective Communication
Anahata	The Unstruck Sound Center	Love	Selfishness
Manipura	The Jewel City Center	Energy	Ego
Svadhisthana	The Support Of The Life Breath Center	Emotional Balance	Desires
Muladhara	The Root Center	Willpower	Survival

RIGHT: ***There are seven major chakra points situated along the length of the spine. They correlate with the endocrine system.***

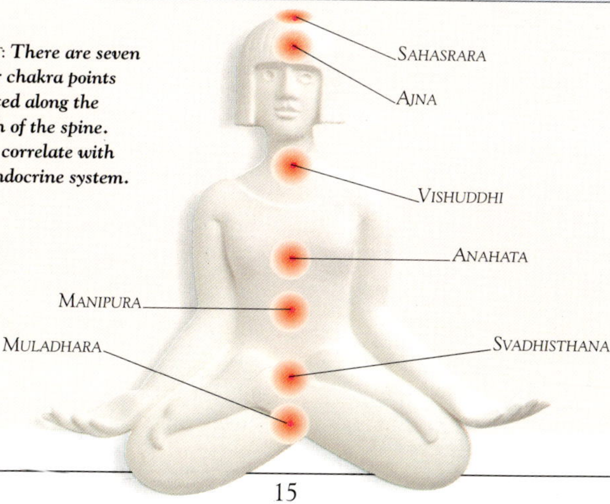

Pranayama ~ the science of breathing

RADIANT HEALTH *is only possible when we are breathing fully and freely. We need plenty of oxygen in order to purify the bloodstream and burn up waste matter.*

ABOVE: ***A crush of commuters! Stress undermines many body functions.***

Amidst the busy, stressful lifestyle of this modern age, human beings have lost the art of correct breathing. Did you know that shallow breathing uses only one-tenth of our lung capacity? That a caved-in chest leads to shallow breathing and retention of tension? Shallow breathing cuts down oxygen intake, and can result in conditions such as fatigue, lack of mental alertness, and headaches.

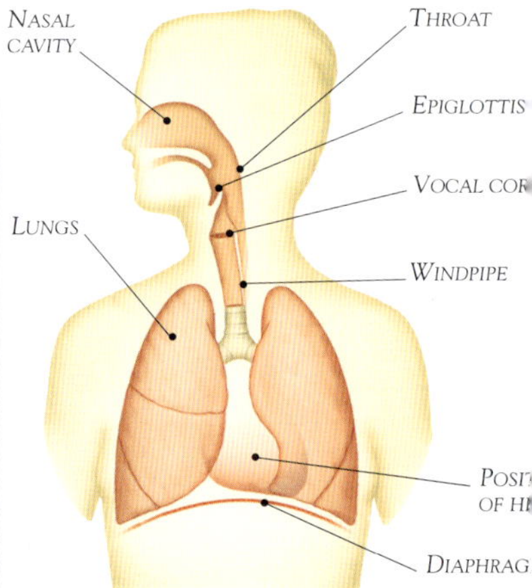

ABOVE: ***Poor posture contributes to preventing the lungs from functioning at optimum levels.***

Most of us don't realize just how great a part breathing ("the breath") plays in energizing the body, considering that there are only two main sources of energy available to us – the food we eat and the air we breathe.

For the yogi, "prana" is his life force, the very power behind the breath. If we can control the breath, therefore, we will be able to access a great reservoir of vital energy.

The word "Pranayama" can be broken into two parts:

- **Prana** – *Life force*
- **Yama** – *Control*

By conscious control of the breath, we can create a proper rhythm of slow, deep breathing. These rhythmical patterns strengthen the respiratory system, soothe the nervous system, reduce craving and desire, free the mind, and improve concentration. Pranayama is therefore a simple means by which we can consciously control our energy and emotional levels.

BELOW: ***Recurrent nagging headaches may be attributed to poor breathing technique.***

ABOVE: ***For opera singers such as Maria Callas, good breathing control is imperative.***

PRANAYAMA

- Deepens breathing
- Stretches the intercostal muscles
- Aids conditions such as asthma
- Calms the mind and emotions
- Helps in the relief of grief and sadness

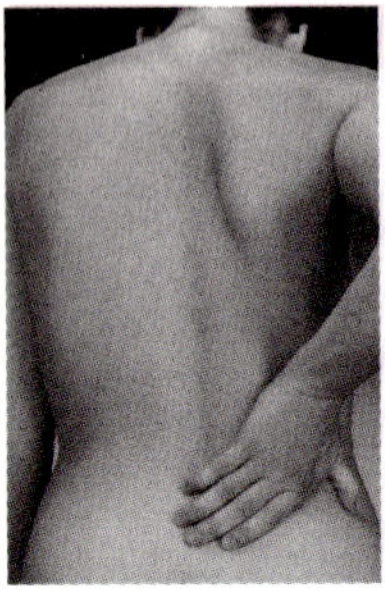

ABOVE: ***Backache is a common problem. It can be improved by some yoga postures.***

Alignment

ALIGNMENT MEANS KEEPING *the body within its own natural range of movements. It is important to allow your body to find its own comfortable limit and not to overstrain or try to achieve more than you are physically able to. Perfection is what you can achieve in any one moment.*

Poor postural habits and poor breathing can result in physical, mental, or emotional difficulties. On the other hand, good body alignment and deep, slow, rhythmic breathing can lead us to improved health and clearer thinking patterns.

In order to enhance and develop your yoga it is useful to structure your practice. The development of awareness is the key. This can be achieved by focusing on:

- which muscles are toned and stretched;
- what is happening to the spine;
- how the breath is moving;
- where your thoughts are;
- what you feel – heat, cold, other sensations.

Try to make these observations before, during, and after your yoga practice. You may even wish to keep a journal to record your experiences.

Once you are able to develop this sensitivity and awareness in your practice, it will begin to influence every moment of your day. Standing at a bus stop, queuing at a supermarket, sitting down to lunch or at a

RIGHT: ***Through constant practice dancers are easily able to achieve perfect balance and alignment.***

meeting, at work or in a car, you will begin to feel your body alignment and your breathing will adjust and/or correct as you go along. In this way you will be practicing yoga all the time.

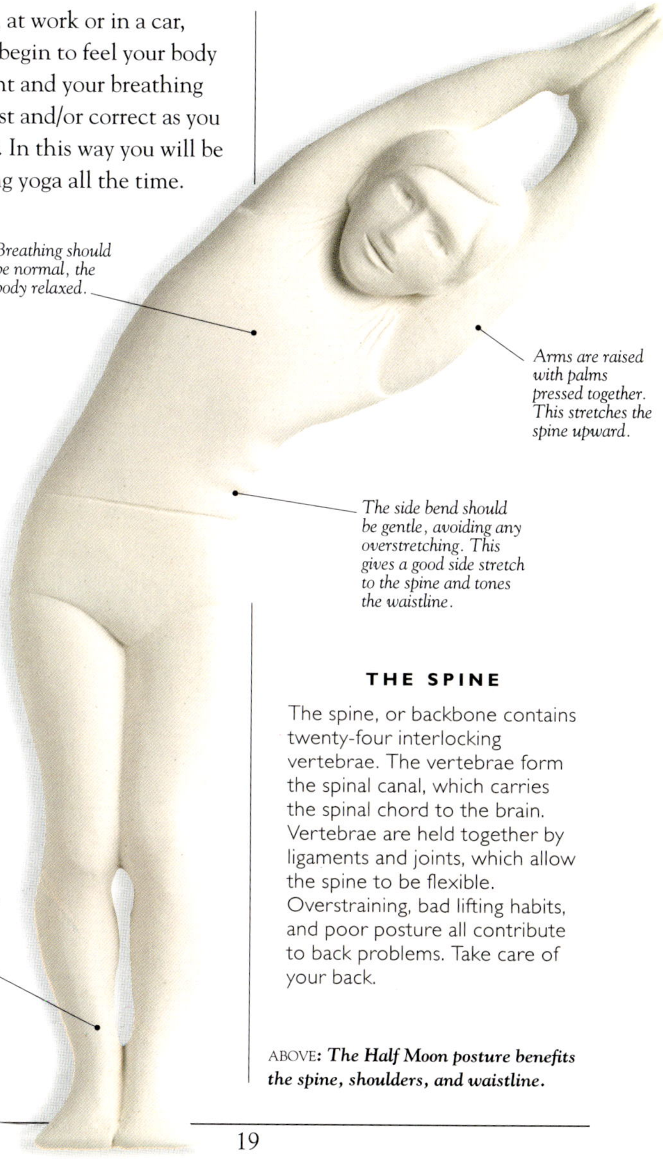

THE SPINE

The spine, or backbone contains twenty-four interlocking vertebrae. The vertebrae form the spinal canal, which carries the spinal chord to the brain. Vertebrae are held together by ligaments and joints, which allow the spine to be flexible. Overstraining, bad lifting habits, and poor posture all contribute to back problems. Take care of your back.

ABOVE: ***The Half Moon posture benefits the spine, shoulders, and waistline.***

Warm~ups

WARM-UPS before you practice are essential. It is particularly important to prepare the muscles if you live in a climate that is not always warm. These simple stretches also warn the muscles that something special is about to take place, thus encouraging maximum benefits from the yoga practice that follows.

Before you begin, it is important to remove accumulated tension from all parts of your body. The following movements will gently stretch your muscles, loosen your joints, and encourage deeper breathing. In this way you will begin to attune yourself with your body and so derive maximum benefit from your practice. Hold the movements for a count of three and gradually increase the length of time as you progress.

We call this six-series exercise an **Energy Block Release**.

1 Stand tall, feet together. Inhale, raising your arms from your sides.

STANDING STRETCH

2 Extend them above your head. Stretch high, raising up on to your toes. Hold for a few moments.

3 Exhale, lower your arms to your sides. Repeat twice more.

SIDE STRETCH

1 Stand tall, arms by your sides. Separate your feet, shoulder-width apart. Inhale, raising your right arm from your side. Extend it above your head, palm facing to the left.

2 Exhale and bend to the left. (Try not to push your right hip out and keep your right shoulder back.) Slide your left arm down your left leg for support. Hold. Inhale, slowly returning to an upright position.

3 Exhale, turn your palm to face out and lower your arm to your side. Repeat on the opposite side.

TWIST

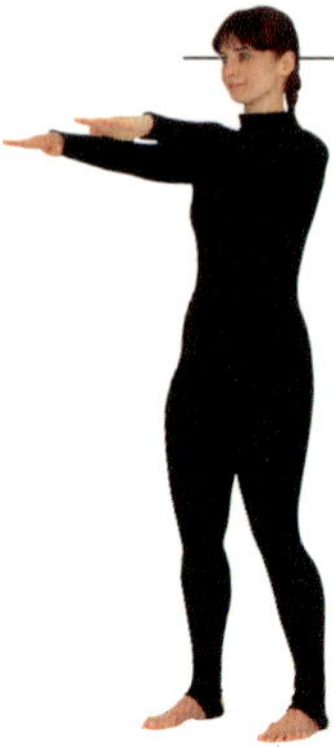

1 *Stand tall, feet hip-width apart. Inhale, raising your arms in front to shoulder height.*

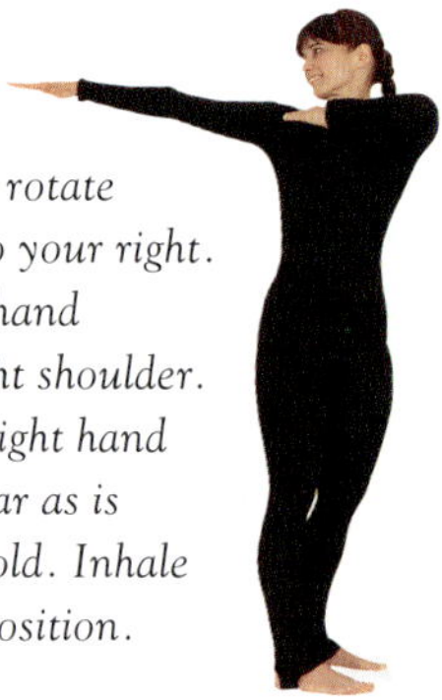

2 *Exhale, and rotate your arms to your right. Draw your left hand toward your right shoulder. Focus on your right hand as you turn as far as is comfortable. Hold. Inhale in this position.*

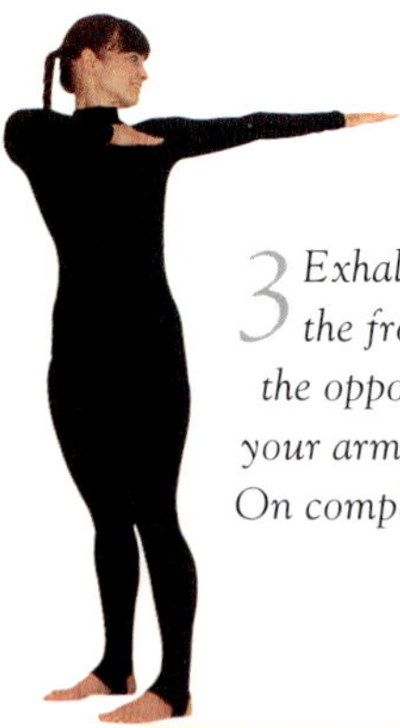

3 *Exhale and return to the front. Repeat on the opposite side. Lower your arms to your sides. On completion, relax.*

CONTRAINDICATIONS

If you suffer from severe back pain, omit this movement.

BACKWARD AND FORWARD BEND

1 *Stand tall, your feet hip-width apart. Place your hands on your hips. Inhale.*

2 *Exhale and bend back. Keep your head facing forward. Inhale and return to upright position.*

3 *Exhale and bend forward. In a comfortable position, release your hands and allow them to hang loosely. Hold and relax.*

4 *Bend knees slightly and uncurl upward vertebra by vertebra, keeping your head relaxed. Return slowly to an upright position.*

SQUAT

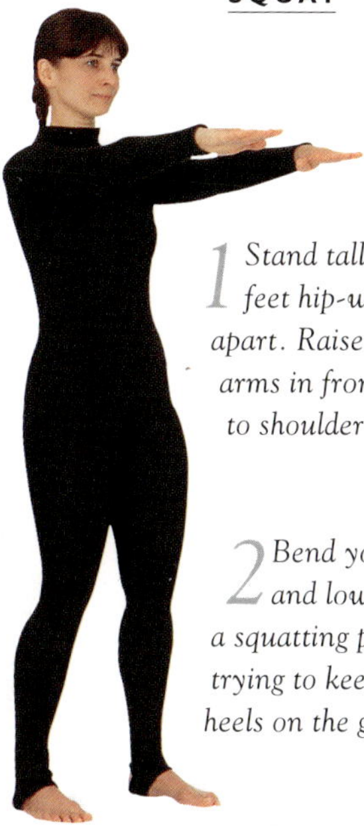

1 Stand tall, your feet hip-width apart. Raise your arms in front of you to shoulder height.

2 Bend your knees and lower into a squatting position, trying to keep your heels on the ground.

LEG EXTENSION

1 Place your hands on the floor as shown. Extend your right leg to the side. Point your toes forward, upward, away.

2 Draw your leg to the center. Repeat on the left side.

3 Return to a standing position, then lower your arms and relax.

Breathing exercises

THE FOLLOWING *are four very useful breathing exercises, designed to encourage deep breathing (Breath of Arjuna), develop total body awareness (Alternate Nostril Breath), increase vitality (Vitality Breath), and improve the power of positive communication (Pigeon Breath).*

THE BREATH OF ARJUNA

1 Stand tall, your feet hip-width apart. Cross one arm in front of the other, holding them in front of your navel.

2 Inhale and raise your arms above your head. Exhale and lower your arms sideways. Repeat three times.

THE BREATH OF ARJUNA

- Opens chest, relaxes shoulders, encourages deep breathing
- Calms mind and emotions
- Improves chest complaints, including asthma and bronchitis
- Overcomes depression and shoulder tension

ALTERNATE NOSTRIL BREATH

1 Sit in a comfortable position on a chair or on the floor.

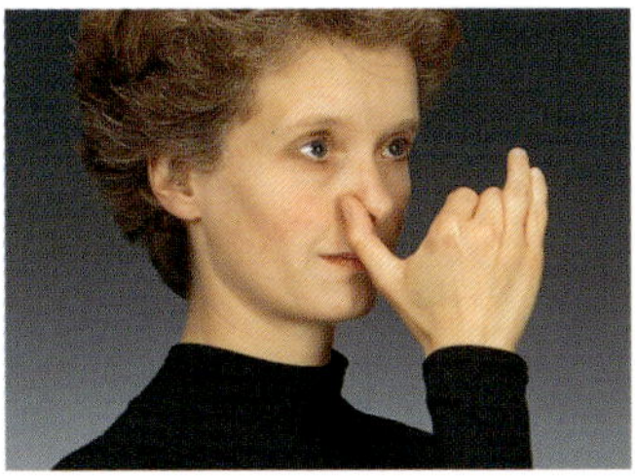

2 Using your right hand, fold your middle and index fingers into your palm. Block your right nostril with your thumb. Inhale through your left nostril.

ALTERNATE NOSTRIL BREATH

- Mind and body balance
- Calms the mind, aids relaxation
- Purifies the nerves
- Develops total body awareness

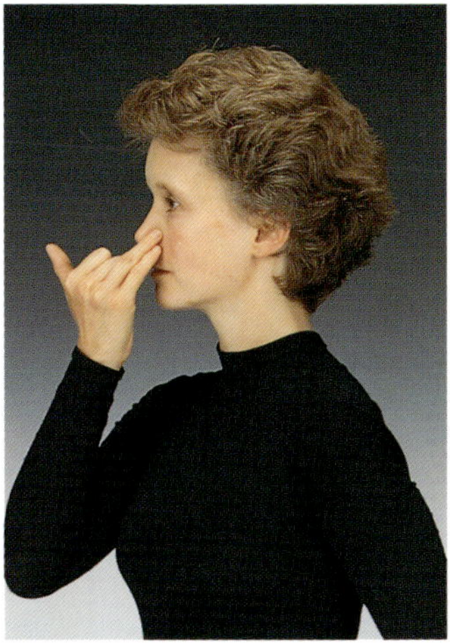

3 Block your left nostril with your little finger and fourth finger. Release your thumb, breathe out through your right nostril. Breathe in through your right nostril.

4 Block your right nostril with your thumb and release your left nostril. Exhale through your left nostril. This completes one cycle. Repeat five to ten times.

Body instruction: Keep head upright. Make sure you do not retain breath at any point. Keep your back straight.

VITALITY BREATH

1 This is a forced breath. Take a deep breath through both your nostrils.

2 Pull in the abdominal muscles and diaphragm in a sharp in-stroke that forces the air out of your nose so fast that it is almost a sneeze. Immediately the exhalation is finished, relax and inhale naturally in a short burst. Exhalation should take less time that inhalation. To begin with, perform the vitality breath ten times at a rate of two exhalations per second. This completes one round. Take a minute's rest between each round. Start with two rounds and build up gradually to five.

Body instruction: Short exhalation. Keep spine straight. Contract your abdominal muscles.

VITALITY BREATH

- Gives vitality
- Increases concentration
- Improves digestive disorders
- Creates a healthy physical body
- Clears the sinuses
- Improves the circulation
- Rejuvenates
- Prolongs life

CONTRAINDICATIONS

This breathing exercise should not be performed during menstruation, or if you have cataracts, hernia, hypertension, or epilepsy.

PIGEON BREATH

1 Stand comfortably with your feet hip-width apart. Interlace your fingers in front of you and place them underneath your chin. Put your elbows together in front of your chest.

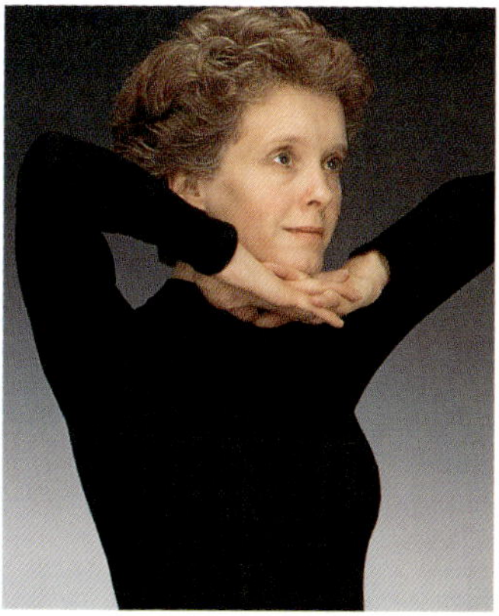

2 Inhale through your nose and lift up your elbows as high as possible. Your chin should now be resting on your hands.

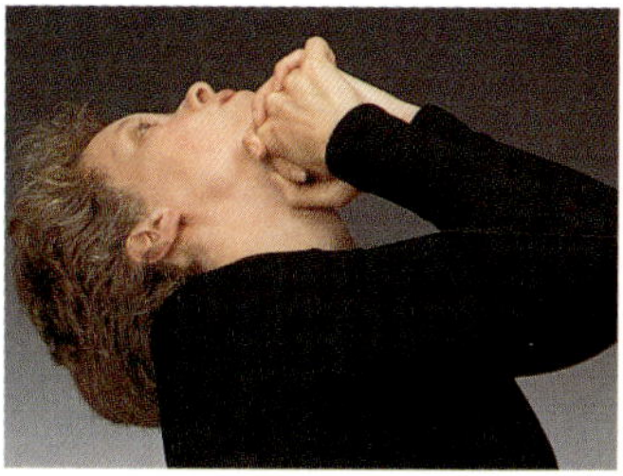

3 Exhale gently through your mouth and at the same time let the hands push the chin upward, while the elbows come forward and touch in front. Inhale in this position. Exhale and allow your hands and elbows to return to the original starting position. Repeat the sequence three to five times.

Benefits: Calms the breath. Slows the breathing. Soothes the nervous system. Exercises the lungs. Stimulates thyroid and parathyroid glands.

CONTRAINDICATIONS

Avoid pushing your head back too far as this might compress vertebrae in the neck. This is especially important for people with epilepsy.

Postures

EACH OF THE POSTURES THAT FOLLOW *is like a special key that will serve to unlock a part of you, releasing a reservoir of untapped energy and potential. Take time to enter into each posture in order to experience the alignment, muscle tone, energy flow, sensations, and thoughts. Observe how you feel before and after each posture. Gradually you will come to know and experience the human body as the miracle it is.*

STANDING POSTURES

THE TREE

1 Stand tall. Tuck the heel of your left foot into the inside of your right thigh, toes pointing down and knee pointing out to side.

2 Extend your arms above your head. Bring your palms together. Hold for 30 seconds. Release your foot and lower your arms. Repeat on the other side.

THE TREE

- Tones leg muscles
- Improves joint flexibility, especially ankle, knee, and shoulders
- Stretches the back muscles
- Opens the chest
- Improves balance and concentration

Body instruction: Tighten the muscles of your supporting leg. Press the side of your foot firmly into your thigh.

CHAIR OF THE HEART

1 Stand tall. Raise your arms from sides. Rotate your palms to face upward at shoulder height.

CHAIR OF THE HEART

- Tones the muscles, back, and legs
- Flexes the ankle, hip, and knee joints
- Opens the chest and heart area

2 Make your palms meet above your head, with your elbows hugging your ears.

3 Begin to bend your knees until they are at an angle of approximately 60 degrees. (Imagine you are sitting on a chair!)

Body instruction:
Heels stay on the ground. Back is straight. Squeeze your shoulder blades together. Stretch your torso up, push your heels down. Flex your ankles. Look ahead. Return to upright position. Lower your arms to your sides. Alternative: arms parallel.

CONTRAINDICATIONS

Heart problems (too much of a strain).

SIDE-BEND POSTURES

THE TRIANGLE

1 Stand tall, your feet approximately 3 feet (1 meter) apart. Rotate your right foot 90 degrees to the right (knee and thigh also). Left foot turns slightly toward right.

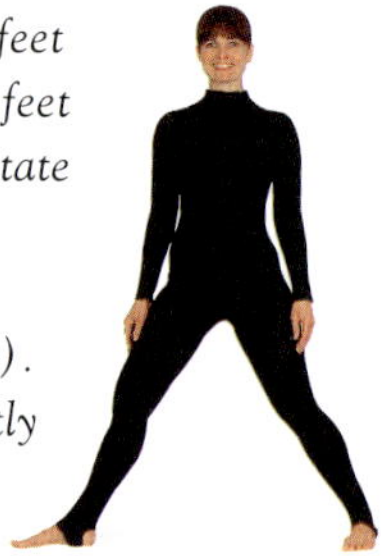

2 Raise your arms to shoulder height, palms facing forward.

CONTRAINDICATIONS

*If there is tension in the neck, omit this movement.

THE TRIANGLE

- Stretches the leg, back, and neck
- Loosens the hips
- Twists the spine
- Increases the circulation
- Improves digestion and elimination

3 Extend your right arm out to the right and lower toward your right ankle. Bend knee if necessary. Left arm is vertical to right arm in one line. Rotate your head to look up. Lower your head. Return to the upright position. Lower your arms down to your side.*

Body instruction: To assist this movement (a) contract thighs and buttocks, and (b) revolve trunk upwards, squeezing shoulder blades. Keep the shoulders and hip back. Rotate the knee and thigh right. Rotate the foot 90 degrees to right. Heel of the right foot is in line with the arch of the left foot. Contract the thighs.

DANCE OF THE LEGS

1 Assume a comfortable position lying down on your back. Extend your arms sideways to shoulder height. Palms face upward.

2 Raise your left leg to the vertical. Bend it at the knee and place your knee on the floor on the right side.

DANCE OF THE LEGS

- Relieves tension in the lower back
- Twists the spine
- Activates the kidneys
- Aids digestion
- Generates energy

Body instruction: Place cushions under your knee and head if necessary. Shoulders stay on the floor. Spine lengthens and twists.

CONTRAINDICATIONS

Omit if you have an acute back condition. Avoid this posture during pregnancy.

3 Rotate your head to the left. Hold. Raise your knee to the vertical. Place your foot on the floor and slide into a relaxed position. Repeat with other leg.

INVERTED POSTURES

SHOULDER STAND

NOTE

Preparation is essential for this posture.

1 Place two or three folded blankets on the floor. Lie with your shoulders and arms on the blankets and your head on the floor. Bend your knees, your feet flat on the floor close to your buttocks.

2 Draw your knees toward your chest. Lift your trunk, using your shoulders not your hands, and push down on your elbows.

3 Placc your palms on your hips and support your torso. Raise your trunk and draw your sternum toward your chin. Move your hands lower to support your back. Straighten your legs until they are vertical. Hold for as long as you are comfortable.

CONTRAINDICATIONS

Avoid Shoulder Stand if you suffer from neck pain, glaucoma, obesity, weak back, and disc problems or during menstruation.

PLOUGH

1 Lower your feet slowly to the floor over your head and hold.

2 To come out of the posture, raise your legs back to the vertical. Release your hands to the floor and use to support movement as you slowly slide back into the lying position. Knees bent, lower your feet to the floor.

PLOUGH

- Rejuvenates the nervous system
- Helps healthy function of the thyroid and parathyroid glands
- Relieves constipation and headaches
- Removes tiredness
- Helps insomnia
- Improves circulation
- Helps varicose veins

Counterpose: the Fish. See page 34.

Body instruction: Tuck in sacrum. Sternum moves toward chin. Stretch spine. Open back of legs. Relax. Soles vertical.

FISH POSTURE

BACK-BEND POSTURES

SIMPLE FISH – COUNTERPOSE FOR SHOULDER STAND

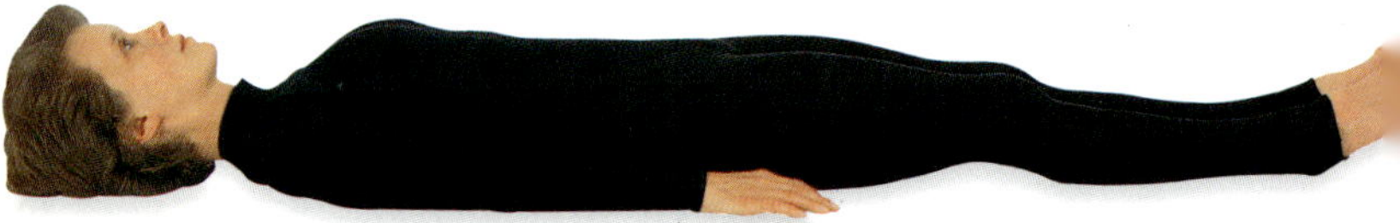

1 Lie down on your back. Place your elbows close to the side of your ribcage, arms flat on the floor and weight on your elbows.

Body instruction: Do not put too much pressure on the crown of the head or the neck. Chest up. Relax legs.

CONTRAINDICATIONS

Do not perform if you have a cervical or serious neck problem.

2 Lift your head and place your crown on the floor, without putting your body weight on your head. Draw your shoulder blades together and hold. To come out of the posture, lift your head slightly and slide on to the floor.

PELVIC LIFT VERSION 1

1 Lie on your back. Bend your knees and draw toward your buttocks, a hip-width apart.

2 Lift your hips off the ground and take hold of your ankles. To come out of the posture, lower gradually, tucking your pelvis in. Repeat twice more.

PELVIC LIFT VERSION 2

1 Place your hands/palms against your back to help lift the torso.

2 Contract your buttocks. Relax your neck and shoulder joint muscles. Chin on chest. To come out of the posture, lower gradually, tucking your pelvis in. Repeat twice more.

Body instruction: Chest moves toward the chin. Keep your shoulders down.

PELVIC LIFT

- Loosens the shoulder joints
- Stretches the arms, legs, abdomen, and neck muscles
- Flexes the spine

CONTRAINDICATIONS

Avoid if you have had a recent operation, or suffer from a serious abdominal disorder, hernia, or high blood-pressure; also during menstruation and pregnancy.

THE COBRA

1 Lie on your front. Place your arms either side of your ribcage, elbows tucked into your sides. Inhale, and slowly raise your head and chest from the floor.

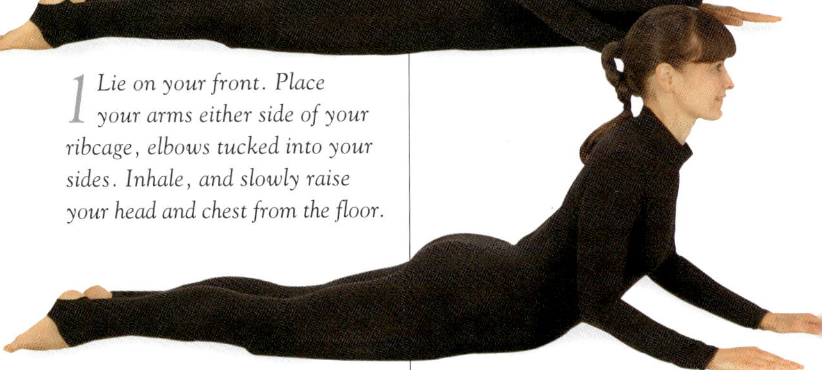

CONTRAINDICATIONS

Avoid the Cobra if suffering from hernia or hypertension.

THE COBRA

- Increases lung capacity
- Strengthens the upper back
- Tones the buttocks
- Stretches the thighs, chest, abdomen
- Strengthens the thyroid
- Improves kidney function
- Flexes the spine
- Increases the efficiency of the organs of digestion and reproduction

2 Straighten your arms, whilst keeping navel on the floor. Stretch your spine up and back. Hold. Exhale, and lower down to the floor.

Body instruction: Push your hips down on to floor. Contract the gluteals (buttocks). Stretch your spine up and back. Head back without compressing vertebrae. Chest forward.

THE CAT

THE CAT

- Strengthens the back and tones the muscles
- Gives flexibility to the spine
- Improves the digestive system

1 Kneel on all fours, your hands shoulder-width apart, knees the same distance as your hands.

2 Exhale and arch your back up high. Your stomach contracts. Your head moves between your arms, your chin to your sternum.

3 Inhale and slowly hollow your back, creating a concave effect. Your head raises to look up. This completes the cycle. Repeat four to five times, creating a slow, flowing rhythm. Movement up or down always begins at the base of the spine and moves along like a wave.

CONTRAINDICATIONS

Do not over-accentuate the curving of the spine if you are pregnant.

Body instruction: Hands directly under your shoulders. Knees directly under your hips. Contract your abdominal muscles. Create a wave-like movement from the base of your spine up to your neck.

FORWARD-BEND POSTURES

PEACE POSTURE

1 Stand tall, your feet hip-width apart. Raise your arms from your sides and extend them above your head, palms facing forward.

PEACE POSTURE

- Stretches the hamstrings and calves
- Elongates the spine
- Activates the kidneys
- Massages the digestive system

CONTRAINDICATIONS

Do not perform the Peace Posture if you have cataracts.

2 Reach forward and lower into the forward bend. Take hold of your ankles or whatever part of your leg you can comfortably reach. Gently draw your head toward your knees. Feel the stretch in your back, kidneys, hamstrings. Release and uncurl from the base of your spine, returning to a standing position.

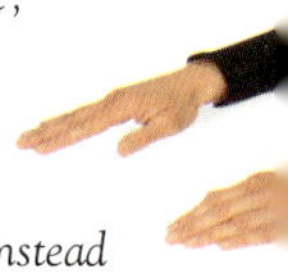

If you have a bad back this may be too strenuous. Instead raise your arms only to shoulder height. Bend forward from the hip with your knees soft, and relax down. Half-way down, take a deep breath. Continue as above.

Body instruction: Try to elongate your spine. Open the back of your legs.

THE CROCODILE

1 Lie on your front. Separate your legs as much as is comfortable, feet facing outward.

2 Interlock your hands on your elbows, placing your forehead to rest on your forearms.

Body instruction: Coccyx tucks in. Feet face out. Feet as far apart as is comfortable.

THE CROCODILE

- Massages the abdomen
- Relaxes the mind
- Aids digestion

TWISTING POSTURES

THE SPINAL TWIST VERSION 1

1 Assume a sitting position on the floor. Extend your legs out in front and bend your knees. Take hold of your left ankle with your right hand.

2 Place your left heel beneath your right thigh. Place your right heel to rest on the floor in front of your left knee.

3 Place your right arm inside your right leg. Clasp the inside right ankle.

Body instruction: Spine straight. Knee pushes into body.

4 Place your left hand on the floor behind your back close to your body, fingers facing away. Inhale, stretching your spine up. Exhale and twist to the left. Don't lean. Hold. Release, and return to face forward. Repeat on the opposite side.

THE SPINAL TWIST VERSION 2

1 Assume a sitting position as before. Place the crease of your left arm around your right knee. Place the palm of your left hand along your right thigh.

2 Place your right arm behind your back close to your body, fingers facing away. Inhale, stretching the spine. Exhale and rotate to the right. Hold. Release and return to front. Repeat on the opposite side.

THE SPINAL TWIST

- Improves back pain
- Improves digestive disorders
- Kidneys, liver, and stomach are massaged
- Aids proper elimination
- Activates adrenals
- Improves energy levels

Body instruction: Spine straight. Knee pushes into body.

CONTRAINDICATIONS

Avoid if you have had a recent operation, or suffer from hernia, severe abdominal disorders, or during pregnancy.

Sequences

SEQUENCES COMPRISE A NUMBER OF *specific postures designed to unlock the body, relax, and create a natural rhythm and flow. Traditionally, it is thought that the individual consists of both male, or sun, and female, or moon, energies. The sun and moon sequences therefore provide a perfect balance for each other. Each sequence has its own unique way of either calming or activating the body/heart/mind connection.*

THE SUN SEQUENCE
Surya Namaskar

The salutation to the sun is a beautiful series of movements that loosen and energize the entire body.

1 *Stand tall, your feet together, your palms touching in front of your chest.*

2 *Inhale and stretch your arms up and back. Tighten your buttocks.*

3 *Exhale, bend forward and place your hands on the floor. Take your head toward your knees. Your legs should be kept straight.*

4 *Inhale and extend your right foot as far back as possible, toes touching the floor. Your left knee is at 90 degrees.*

5 *Exhale and draw your left foot back to meet the right. Your head, back and legs should form a straight line. Hold your breath.**

6 Turn your hands in slightly, bending your arms and knees so that your toes, knees, chest, hands, and chin are touching the floor.

*7 Inhale, straightening your arms as you bend backward, your lower body resting on the floor.**

8 Exhale and raise your hips into the air. Your hands and feet should stay on the floor.

9 Inhale. Bring your right foot forward, knee to chest, and raise your face to look up.

10 Exhale. Draw your left foot to join the right. Draw your head to your chest. Keep your legs straight.

*11 Inhale. Raise your arms above your head and bend backward.**

12 Exhale and draw your arms together in front of your chest.

Practice: Perform the whole sequence twice and relax on completion for a few minutes. You may increase the number of rounds with practice.

CONTRAINDICATIONS

*Omit the back bend if you suffer from chronic back pain. Do not hold the breath if you have high blood-pressure or suffer from epilepsy.

THE MOON SEQUENCE
Chandra Namaskar

The moon affects our emotional body, and the practice of this sequence helps to balance and control the emotions and the hormones.

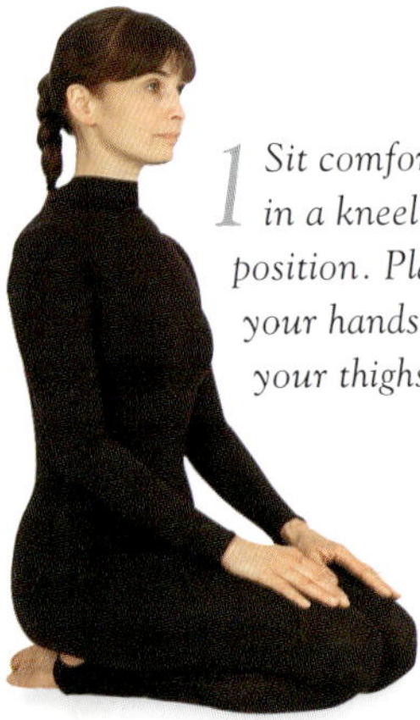

1 *Sit comfortably in a kneeling position. Place your hands on your thighs.*

2 *Lightly press your palms together in front of your chest.*

3 *Raise yourself up on to your knees.*

4 *Place your right foot on to the floor in front, creating an angle of 90 degrees.*

5 *Inhale, and as you exhale extend your arms forward.*

6 Inhale, and extend your arms either side at shoulder height.

7 Exhale, and lower your right hand to rest on the floor on the outside of your right foot. Inhale, and raise your head to look up. Exhale, and lower your head. Inhale, and raise your arms to the upright position.

8 Exhale and lower your left arm, placing it on the floor on the inside of your right foot.

9 Inhale, and look up. Exhale, and look down.

10 Inhale, and return to a kneeling position.

11 Raise your right leg, exhale, and rotate your palms to face upward.

12 Inhale, and extend your arms above your head, palms touching.

13 Exhale. Lower your arms to the front at chest level.

14 Inhale, and draw your praying hands toward your chest. Return to the kneeling position.

15 Place your palms on the floor.

THE MOON SEQUENCE

- Activates kidneys
- Removes fear and fatigue
- Opens the chest
- Twists the spine and strengthens the back

16 Extend your legs back to form a press-up position.

17 Lower on to the floor.

18 Place your palms either side of your shoulders, fingers facing forward.

19 Inhale. Raise your head and chest from the floor, keeping your navel on the floor. Tuck your elbows into your chest. Exhale and lower.

20 Push back into child posture. Raise up into kneeling posture. Repeat one to fifteen times.

Relaxation

*A*T THE END *of your practice it is important to take 5–10 minutes to relax your body. Relaxation is a state of total receptivity where, through deep breathing, the body can replenish and rejuvenate itself as the natural potential of the body to heal itself comes into play. It is an opportunity to release any pockets of tension in the muscles and improve oxygen exchange within the body, thus creating a greater source of energy potential. In order to relax, it is necessary to concentrate the mind. Soft, relaxing music can help to create a conducive atmosphere.*

ABOVE: ***Make yourself comfortable on a rug. You may find that covering yourself with a blanket will aid relaxation.***

3-MINUTE RELAXATION

1 Inhale and tighten your toes, calves, thighs, and buttocks.

2 Exhale and relax.

3 Inhale, expanding your abdomen and chest.

4 Exhale and relax back on to the floor.

5 Inhale and stretch out your hands, arms, and shoulders.

6 Exhale and relax.

7 Inhale, contracting your facial muscles.

8 Exhale and relax.

9 On the next exhalation allow your whole body to relax.

10 Stretch and awaken your body when you are ready.

10-MINUTE VISUALIZATION

Simply lie down and visualize that your body has come to rest on a beautiful warm beach. Feel the warmth of the sun above you, deeply relaxing your body as it sinks heavily into the warm sand. Imagine you can hear the waves lapping on the shore, soothing your mind, and the sweet sound of birds flying above, while the smell of fresh warm air fills your body. Relax, relax, relax.

Awaken yourself by drawing a fresh revitalizing breath into every part of your body. Stretch and awaken.

RIGHT: ***The pose of tranquillity shown here and on page 48, is a good position for relaxing. After the period of relaxation, avoid eating for at least 30 minutes.***

Meditation

MEDITATION IS THE KEY *to success. It provides a tool to harness and control the greatest source of power we possess as human beings – the mind.*

RIGHT: ***The final part of the peace mudra, which helps you to achieve a deep level of inner peace.***

The practice of yoga is a stepping stone toward successful meditation: the quietening of the mind and the stilling of thoughts. Meditation takes us beyond the restless activity of the mind to a deeper, more peaceful space. Through contemplation and meditation we can gain new perspectives on life and fill our body and mind with energy. It puts us in touch with our true nature, which is joy and love. We could spend a whole lifetime seeking outside ourselves for happiness, but in reality it can only be found inside, for within us lies the secret to life itself.

PEACE MUDRA

1 Sit comfortably on a chair or on the floor. Place your hands on your knees, palms upward.

2 On taking your next breath, turn fingers inward toward the base of the abdomen, holding them just away from the body.

3 Draw the hands up to the level of the diaphragm. Exhale.

4 Turn hands toward the body, palms facing up, little fingers close to the body, and thumbs furthest away.

5 Inhale and raise palms up to throat level. Exhale and turn palms to face the throat.

6 Inhale and raise your hands, extending them sideways above your head. Exhale and hold for as long as is comfortable. On exhalation, lower palms in three stages as above. Relax hands on to the knees and reflect on the word "peace."

CANDLE-GAZING

1 Place a candle on a small table in front of you.

2 Maintain your gaze for as long as comfortable.

3 Close your eyes and imagine the flame behind your eyes.

4 Hold the image.

5 Repeat two or three times.

6 Relax your eyes and sit quietly for another 10 minutes. Gradually try to lengthen the time you sit for up to 20 minutes.

BELOW: ***Candle-gazing improves concentration and assists in meditation. It also helps relax you.***

CAUTION

Make sure the candle is safely placed so it cannot fall over. Never leave a burning candle unattended.

Establishing a personal daily program

THE SECRET of yoga is regular practice. Build up your routine gradually and it will change your life.

ABOVE: ***The knee and thigh stretch is said to help keep the urinary system in good order.***

A regular practice is most important, for it frees the latent forces of the body, bringing a natural immunity to illness and the chaos of life. If you commit yourself to a regular yoga practice, we guarantee that your life will be transformed within eighteen days. The optimum times to practice are in the morning straight after rising, and/or after returning from work, or just before you go to sleep at night. The exercises are arranged here in weekly groups, to provide a carefully graded course of yoga.

TO ENHANCE YOUR PRACTICE

- Wear comfortable clothing.
- Practice at least 2 hours after a full meal.
- Practice in a warm room.
- It is important not to strain or exceed your body's natural capacity.
- Take your time and enjoy yourself.
- Take the phone off the hook.

N.B. If you suffer from an acute condition you may wish to consult a physician or experienced yoga teacher before practicing.

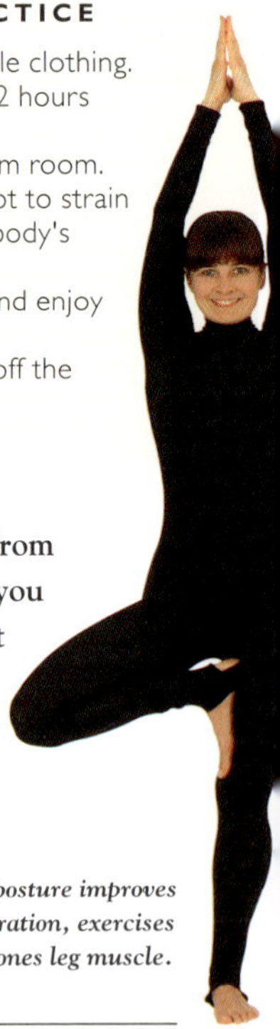

RIGHT: ***the Tree posture improves balance and concentration, exercises the joints and tones leg muscle.***

The structure provided here is a simple guide for use until you have established a form of practice which suits YOU and your needs. Try to include a warm-up beforehand, and relaxation after the session, as part of any practice.

WEEKLY PLANNER

Week 1
- Energy Block Release
- Breath of Arjuna
- Peace Posture
- Relaxation
- Meditation

Week 2
- Energy Block Release
- Vitality Breath
- Triangle
- Moon Sequence
- Relaxation
- Meditation

Week 3
- Energy Block Release
- Breath of Arjuna
- Sun Sequence
- Tree
- Twist
- Shoulder Stand and Plough
- Fish
- Alternate Nostril Breath
- Relaxation
- Meditation

Week 4
- Energy Block Release
- Pigeon Breath
- Moon Sequence
- Tree
- Twist
- Shoulder Stand and Plough
- Fish
- Relaxation
- Alternate Nostril Breath
- Meditation

Week 5
- Energy Block Release
- Sun Sequence
- Chair of the Heart
- Tree
- Cat
- Twist
- Shoulder Stand and Plough
- Fish
- Relaxation
- Alternate Nostril Breath
- Meditation

If time is short, try the following warm-ups
Morning: Sun Salute
Evening: Peace Posture, Cobra or Dog, Shoulder Stand and Plough, Fish, Relaxation

Common ailments

REGULAR PRACTICE *of yoga can greatly improve your health at every level. We have found specific programs to be very beneficial for the following conditions. If, however, you suffer from a serious illness or injury please make sure that you consult your physician or an experienced yoga teacher before beginning any program of yoga movements.*

CIRCULATION

- Sun Salute *p.42*
- Alternate Nostril Breath *p.25*
- Relaxation *p.48*

ALTERNATE NOSTRIL BREATH

HIGH BLOOD-PRESSURE

- Forward Bend *p.22*
- Moon Sequence *p.44*
- Alternate Nostril Breath *p.25*
- Meditation *p.50*

LOW BLOOD-PRESSURE

- Relaxation *p.48*
- Vitality Breath *p.26*
- Shoulder Stand *p.32*
- Plough *p.33*

PLOUGH

HEART DISEASE

- Chair of the Heart *p.29*
- Triangle *p.30*
- Moon Sequence *p.44*
- Alternate Nostril Breath *p.25*

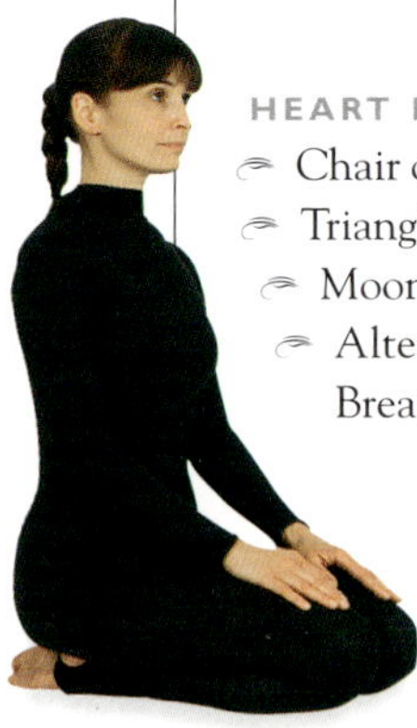

MOON SEQUENCE

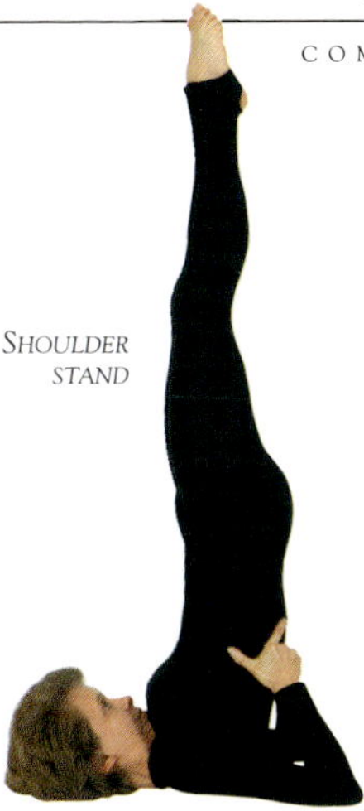

SHOULDER STAND

VARICOSE VEINS

- Shoulder Stand *p.32*
- Fish *p.34*

ASTHMA AND BRONCHITIS

- Breath of Arjuna *p.24*
- Vitality Breath *p.26*
- Shoulder Stand *p.32*
- Fish *p.34*
- Relaxation *p.48*

BREATH OF ARJUNA

COLDS/SINUSES

- Vitality Breath *p.26*
- Breath of Arjuna *p.24*

PIGEON BREATH

ULCERS

- Pigeon Breath *p.27*
- Breath of Arjuna *p.24*
- Relaxation *p.48*
- Meditation *p.50*

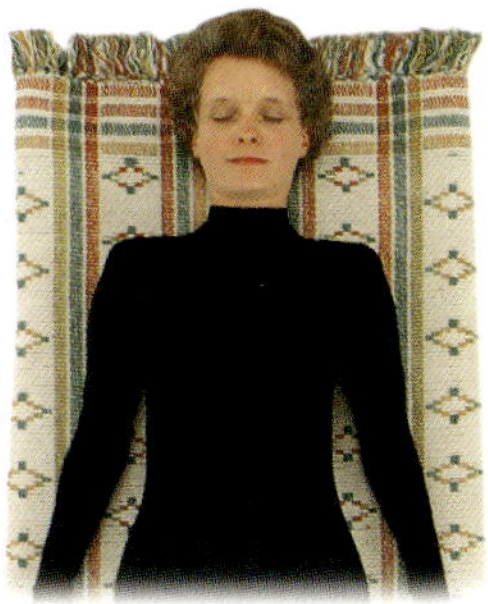

RELAXATION

INDIGESTION

- Vitality Breath *p.26*
- Sun Salute *p.42*
- Spinal Twist *p.40*
- Relaxation *p.48*

CONSTIPATION

- Vitality Breath *p.26*
- Tree *p.28*
- Cobra *p.36*

THE TREE

EPILEPSY

- Fish *p.34*
- Alternate Nostril Breath – no breath retention *p.25*
- Meditation *p.50*

MOON SEQUENCE

ANXIETY

- Breath of Arjuna *p.24*
- Tree *p.28*
- Moon Sequence *p.44*
- Alternate Nostril Breath *p.25*

ANGER

- Spinal Twist *p.40*
- Alternate Nostril Breath *p.25*
- Crocodile *p.39*
- Relaxation *p.48*

CROCODILE

DEPRESSION

- Breath of Arjuna *p.24*
- Chair of the Heart *p.29*
- Moon Sequence *p.44*

FEAR

- Forward Bend *p.22*
- Moon Sequence *p.44*

FATIGUE

- Forward Bend *p.22*
- Cobra *p.36*
- Moon Sequence *p.44*

FORWARD BEND

INSOMNIA

- Moon Sequence *p.44*
- Breath of Arjuna *p.24*
- Shoulder Stand *p.32*
- Fish *p.34*

MOON SEQUENCE

COBRA

HEADACHE

- Energy Block Release *p.20*
- Cat *p.37*
- Cobra *p.36*

SCIATICA

- Tree *p.28*
- Cobra *p.36*
- Backward Bend *p.22*
- Crocodile *p.39*

SHOULDER TENSION

- Warm-ups *pp.20-23*
- Breath of Arjuna *p.24*
- Peace Posture *p.38*

PEACE POSTURE

BACK PAIN

- Cat *p.37*
- Pelvic Lift *p.35*
- Dance of the Legs *p.31*
- Relaxation *p.48*

DANCE OF THE LEGS

ENERGY BLOCK RELEASE

RHEUMATISM AND ARTHRITIS

- Energy Block Release *p.20*
- Cat *p.37*
- Relaxation *p.48*

CAT

DIABETES

- Sun Sequence *p.42*
- Standing Stretch *p.20*
- Cobra *p.36*
- Spinal Twist *p.40*

SUN SEQUENCE

MENSTRUAL DISORDERS

- Breath of Arjuna *p.24*
- Alternate Nostril Breath *p.25*
- Moon Sequence *p.44*

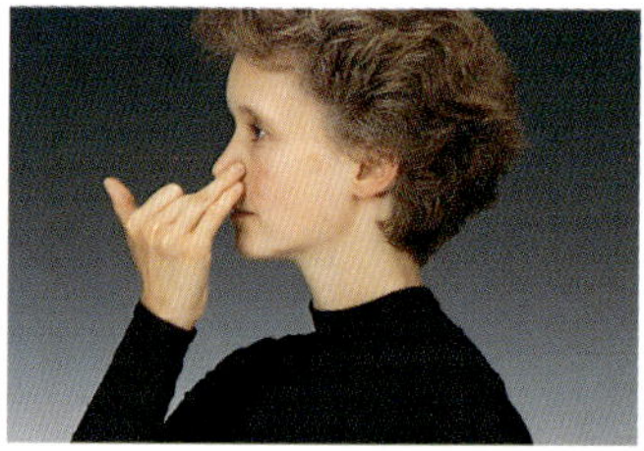

ALTERNATE NOSTRIL BREATH

WEIGHT LOSS

- Sun Salute *p.42*
- Moon Salute *p.44*
- Relaxation *p.48*

SUN SALUTE

Note: All the above suggestions may be optimized by the addition of a warm-up at the beginning and a relaxation at the end.

Further reading

LIFE FOUNDATION PUBLICATIONS: THE DANCE BETWEEN JOY AND PAIN by *Dr Mansukh Patel* and *Rita Goswami* (reprinted 1997)

PREPARING FOR BIRTH WITH YOGA by *Janet Balaskas, Sandra Sabatini* and *Dr Yehudi Gordon* (Element Books, 1994)

THE CRISIS AND THE MIRACLE OF LOVE by *Dr Mansukh Patel* and *Dr Helena Waters* (1997)

YOGA AT WORK by *Miriam Freedman and Janice Hankes* (Element Books, 1996)

BALANCED YOGA by *Dr Svami Purma* (Element Books, 1990)

Useful addresses

Associated Life Project (America)
c/o Jeanne Katz (Independent)
5004 Sunsuite TR.S
Colorado Springs
Colorado 80917
USA

International Training Centre
Snowdon Lodge
Nant Ffrancon
Ty-n-y-Maes
Bethesda
Gwynedd LL57 3LX

International Yoga Teacher's Association
c/o 14/15 Huddart Avenue
Normanhurst
NSW 20766
Australia

Life Foundation School of Therapeutics (Netherlands)
c/o Savitri
Post Bus 88
6670 AB/ZETTEN
Netherlands

Life Foundation School of Therapeutics (UK)
Registered Office:
Maristowe House
Dover Street
West Midlands WV14 6AL

Yoga Centre
Church Farm House
Spring Close Lane
Cheam
Surrey SM3 8PU

Other step-by-step guides
in the Nutshell Series

THE ALEXANDER TECHNIQUE

ALTERNATIVE MEDICINE

AROMATHERAPY

CHINESE HERBAL MEDICINE

HERBAL MEDICINE

HOMEOPATHY

MASSAGE

NATURAL HOME REMEDIES

REFLEXOLOGY

SHIATSU

VITAMINS & MINERALS